I0448447

December 2013

BORDER SECURITY

DHS's Efforts to Modernize Key Enforcement Systems Could be Strengthened

GAO-14-62

BORDER SECURITY

DHS's Efforts to Modernize Key Enforcement Systems Could be Strengthened

Highlights of GAO-14-62, a report to congressional requesters

Why GAO Did This Study

DHS's border enforcement system, known as TECS, is the primary system available for determining admissibility of persons to the United States. It is used to prevent terrorism, and provide border security and law enforcement, case management, and intelligence functions for multiple federal, state, and local agencies. It has become increasingly difficult and expensive to maintain because of technology obsolescence and its inability to support new mission requirements. Accordingly, in 2008, DHS began an effort to modernize the system. It is being managed as two separate programs working in parallel by CBP and ICE.

GAO's objectives were to (1) determine the scope and status of the two TECS Mod programs, (2) assess selected CBP and ICE program management practices for TECS Mod, and (3) assess the extent to which DHS is executing effective executive oversight and governance of the two TECS Mod programs.

To do so, GAO reviewed requirements documents and cost and schedule estimates, and determined the current scope, completion dates, and life cycle expenditures. GAO also reviewed risk management and requirements management plans, as well as governance bodies' meeting minutes.

What GAO Recommends

GAO is recommending DHS improve its efforts to manage requirement and risk, as well as its governance of the TECS Mod programs. DHS agreed with all but one of GAO's eight recommendations, and described actions planned and underway to address them.

View GAO-14-62. For more information, contact David A. Powner at (202) 512-9286 or pownerd@gao.gov.

What GAO Found

Customs and Border Protection (CBP) has defined the scope for its TECS (not an acronym) modernization (TECS Mod) program, but its schedule and cost continue to change; while Immigration and Customs Enforcement (ICE) is overhauling the scope, schedule, and cost of its program after discovering that its initial solution is not technically viable. CBP's $724 million program intends to modernize the functionality, data, and aging infrastructure of legacy TECS and move it to DHS's data centers. CBP plans to develop, deploy, and implement these capabilities between 2008 and 2015. To date, CBP has deployed functionality to improve its secondary inspection processes to air and sea ports of entry and, more recently, to land ports of entry in 2013. However, CBP is in the process of revising its schedule baseline for the second time in under a year. Further, portions of CBP's schedule remain undefined and the program does not have a fully developed master schedule. These factors increase the risk of CBP not delivering TECS Mod by its 2015 deadline. Regarding ICE's $818 million TECS Mod program, it is redesigning and replanning its program, having determined in June 2013 that its initial solution was not viable and could not support ICE's needs. As a result, ICE halted development and is now assessing design alternatives and will revise its schedule and cost estimates. Program officials stated the revisions will be complete in December 2013. Until ICE completes the replanning effort, it is unclear what functionality it will deliver, when it will deliver it, or what it will cost to do so, thus putting it in jeopardy of not completing the modernization by its 2015 deadline.

CBP and ICE have managed many risks in accordance with some leading practices, but they have had mixed results in managing requirements for their programs. In particular, neither program identified all known risks and escalated them for timely management review. Further, CBP's guidance defines key practices associated with effectively managing requirements, but important requirements development activities were underway before these practices were established. ICE, meanwhile, operated without requirements management guidance for years, and its requirements activities were mismanaged as a result. For example, ICE did not complete work on 2,600 requirements in its initial release, which caused testing failures and the deferral and deletion of about 70 percent of its original requirements. ICE issued requirements guidance in March 2013 that is consistent with leading practices, but it has not yet been implemented.

The Department of Homeland Security's (DHS) governance bodies have taken actions to oversee the two TECS Mod programs that are generally aligned with leading practices. Specifically, DHS's governance bodies have monitored TECS Mod performance and progress and have ensured that corrective actions have been identified and tracked. However, the governance bodies' oversight has been based on sometimes incomplete or inaccurate data, and therefore the effectiveness of these efforts is limited. For example, one oversight body rated CBP's program as moderately low risk, based partially on the program's use of earned value management, even though program officials stated that neither they nor their contractor had this capability. Until these governance bodies base their performance reviews on timely, complete, and accurate data, they will be constrained in their ability to effectively provide oversight.

_____ United States Government Accountability Office

Contents

Figures

Abbreviations

CBP	U.S. Customs and Border Protection
CIO	Chief Information Officer
DHS	Department of Homeland Security
ICE	Immigration and Customs Enforcement
IT	information technology
PARM	Office of Program Accountability and Risk Management
TECS Mod	TECS Modernization

December 5, 2013

The Honorable Thomas R. Carper
Chairman
The Honorable Tom Coburn, M.D.
Ranking Member
Committee on Homeland Security and Governmental Affairs
United States Senate

The Honorable Susan M. Collins
United States Senate

The Honorable Michael McCaul
Chairman
Committee on Homeland Security
House of Representatives

The Honorable Jeff Duncan
Chairman
Subcommittee on Oversight and Management Efficiency
Committee on Homeland Security
House of Representatives

The Department of Homeland Security's (DHS) border enforcement system, known as TECS (not an acronym),[1] is used for preventing terrorism, providing border security and law enforcement, and sharing information about people who are inadmissible or may pose a threat to the security of the United States. Originally developed in the 1980s, TECS provides traveler processing and screening, investigations, case management, and intelligence functions for multiple federal, state, and local agencies. Over time, it has become increasingly difficult and expensive to maintain because of technology obsolescence and its inability to support new mission requirements. DHS estimates that TECS's licensing and maintenance costs are expected to be $40 million

---

[1] TECS was created as a system of the Customs Service, which was then a component within the Department of the Treasury. The term TECS initially was the abbreviation for the Treasury Enforcement Communications System. When the Customs Service became part of DHS under the Homeland Security Act, TECS became a DHS system, and thereafter has simply been known as TECS.

to $60 million per year in 2015. In 2008 the department initiated TECS Modernization (TECS Mod) to modernize existing system functionality, address known capability gaps, and move the program's infrastructure to DHS's new data centers. TECS Mod is managed as two separate programs working in parallel: U.S. Customs and Border Protection (CBP) and Immigration and Customs Enforcement (ICE) are each modernizing legacy functionality specific to their respective roles and missions within the department. Both programs intend to be fully operational by September 2015.

Our objectives for this review were to (1) determine the scope and status of the two TECS Mod programs, (2) assess selected CBP and ICE program management practices for TECS Mod, and (3) assess the extent to which DHS is executing effective executive oversight and governance of the two TECS Mod programs.

To address our objectives, we reviewed documentation from both programs, including requirements documents and program cost and schedule estimates, and determined what the current program scope, completion dates, and life-cycle expenditures were expected to be for each program. To assess selected CBP and ICE program management practices for the programs, we examined program documentation, such as risk management and requirements management plans and processes, and compared them to relevant guidance from leading practitioners, such as the Carnegie Mellon University's Software Engineering Institute,[2] assessed program-identified risks/issues and mitigation plans to determine whether risk is being effectively managed; and examined requirements documentation to determine the extent to which stakeholder requirements have been effectively integrated into program capabilities. To assess the extent to which DHS is executing effective executive oversight and governance of the two TECS Mod programs, we analyzed documentation such as executive steering committee meeting minutes and compared meeting results to relevant guidance such as our Information Technology Investment Management

---

[2]See Carnegie Mellon University's Software Engineering Institute, *Capability Maturity Model ® Integration for Development, Version 1.3* (CMMI-Dev, V1.3) (November 2010).

Framework[3] to determine to what extent DHS's governance bodies are providing effective oversight.

We conducted this performance audit from December 2012 to September 2013, in accordance with generally accepted government auditing standards. Those standards require that we plan and perform the audit to obtain sufficient, appropriate evidence to provide a reasonable basis for our findings and conclusions based on our audit objectives. We believe that the evidence obtained provides a reasonable basis for our findings and conclusions based on our audit objectives. Details on our objectives, scope, and methodology can be found in appendix I.

Background

DHS's mission is to lead the unified national effort to secure the United States by preventing and deterring terrorist attacks and protecting against and responding to threats and hazards to the nation. As part of that mission, DHS is responsible for ensuring that the nation's borders are safe and secure, that they welcome lawful immigrants and visitors, and that they promote the free flow of commerce. Within the department, CBP is responsible for customs, immigration, and agricultural processing at ports of entry.[4] ICE is responsible for the investigation and enforcement of border control, customs, and immigration laws.

Overview of the TECS System

TECS is an information technology (IT) and data management system that supports DHS's core border enforcement mission. According to CBP, it is one of the largest, most important law enforcement systems currently in use, and is the primary system available to CBP officers and agents from other departments for use in determining the admissibility of persons wishing to enter the country. In addition, it provides an investigative case management function for activities carried out by ICE agents, including money-laundering tracking and reporting; telephone data analysis; and intelligence reporting and dissemination.

---

[3]GAO, *Information Technology Investment Management A Framework for Assessing and Improving Process Maturity, Version 1.1,* GAO-04-394G (Washington, D.C.: March 2004).

[4]Ports of entry are government-designated locations where CBP inspects persons and goods to determine whether they may be lawfully admitted into the country.

Over time, TECS has evolved into a multifaceted computing platform that CBP describes as a system of systems. This mainframe-based system interfaces with over 80 systems from within DHS, and federal departments and their component agencies, as well as state, local, and foreign governments. It contains over 350 database tables, queries and reports (e.g., querying law enforcement records to determine if a traveler appears on a terrorist watch list), and multiple applications (e.g., ICE's existing investigative case management system). CBP agents and other users access TECS via dedicated terminals. The system is managed by CBP's Office of Passenger Systems Program Office and is currently hosted at CBP's datacenter.

By 2015, CBP estimates that TECS will contain over 1.1 terabytes[5] of data, including over 46 million lookout records—nearly 25 million records relating to the travel documents of permanent residents and refugees, and the border-crossing history for close to a billion travelers. On a daily basis, the system is used by over 70,000 users and handles more than 2 million transactions—including the screening of over 900,000 visitors and approximately 465,000 vehicles every day. In addition, federal, state, local, and international law enforcement entities use TECS to create and disseminate alerts and other law enforcement information about "persons of interest." Ten federal departments and their numerous component agencies access the system to perform a part of their missions. Figure 1 shows the federal departments and component agencies that use TECS. Appendix III contains a description of the key systems and data resident on the existing (legacy) platform.

---

[5]A terabyte is about 1 trillion bytes, or 1,000 gigabytes.

Figure 1: Federal Departments and Component Agencies that Use TECS

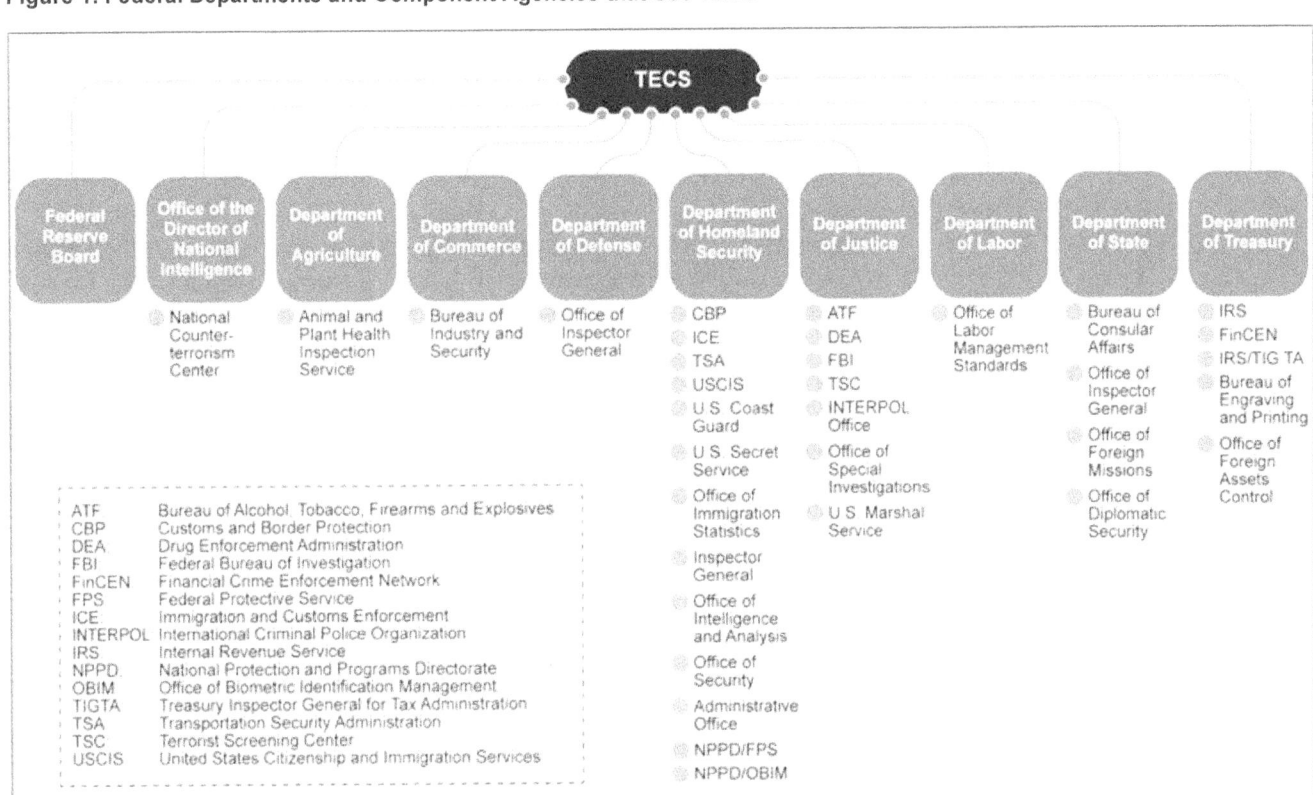

Source: GAO analysis of DHS data

The current TECS system uses obsolete technology, which combined with growing mission requirements, have posed operational challenges for CBP and others. For example, users may need to access and navigate among several different systems to investigate, resolve, and document an encounter with a passenger. In addition, CBP identified that TECS' search algorithms do not adequately match names from foreign alphabets. TECS' obsolescence also makes it difficult and expensive to maintain and support. For example, DHS estimates that TECS's licensing and maintenance costs are expected to be $40 million to $60 million per year in 2015.

Overview of TECS Modernization, Management Structure, and Acquisition Approach

In 2008, DHS initiated efforts to modernize TECS capability by replacing the mainframe technology, developing new applications and enhancing existing applications to address expanding traveler screening mission needs, improving data integration to provide enhanced search and case management capabilities, and improving user interface and data access. DHS plans to migrate away from the existing TECS mainframe by September 2015 to avoid significantly escalating support costs.

The modernization effort is managed by two program offices—CBP and ICE—working in parallel, with each having assumed responsibility for modernizing the parts of the system aligned with their respective missions. CBP's modernization program office organizationally resides within its Office of Information and Technology's Passenger Systems Program Office. This office is responsible for systems that support DHS's and CBP's screening and processing of travelers at U.S. ports of entry, including TECS. ICE's TECS modernization program office resides within ICE's Office of Chief Information Officer. It is responsible for modernizing ICE's IT systems, adapting and conforming to modern IT management disciplines, and providing IT solutions throughout ICE. Homeland Security Investigations Executive Steering Committee provides oversight to the ICE TECS Mod program, including approval and prioritization of requirements, functionality, and decisions on cost, schedule, and performance.

As of July 2013, CBP's program office consisted of approximately 80 staff, split roughly evenly between government and contractor staff, and ICE's program office consisted of about 74 staff—of which 19 are government and 55 are contractors.

In June 2008, CBP awarded a 1-year development contract for its modernization program. From 2009 to 2012, CBP continued its relationship with the same contractor, but awarded a different contract for development services across a range of CBP IT programs. This contract was managed by the Passenger Systems Program Office. The development contractor is to provide, among other things, requirements analysis, system development, and testing; system component migration from development to testing and subsequently to production; operation and maintenance; technical reviews participation; and the development of related documentation as needed. CBP exercised its options on this contract from 2009 to 2012. In January 2013, CBP had issued a new contract for development services, but canceled the award shortly thereafter to make revisions. CBP officials said that the program continues to move forward with plans to complete the development contract award and plans to award the new contract during the fall of 2013. Until then, CBP is continuing to work with the existing contractor. In addition, CBP also contracted separately with other vendors for computer hardware (e.g., servers), as well as for program management support, financial support services, and communications services.

The ICE program office's contracting strategy includes the government as the primary integrator of multiple contractors. ICE awarded its development contract in September 2011. The contract was a 1-year contract with four 1-year option years. The development contractor is to provide, among other things, software design and development services, testing services, information security controls, and technical support. In addition, ICE has established separate contracts for training, data migration, and program management support.

DHS Governance and Oversight of Major IT Programs

DHS's Office of the Chief Information Officer (CIO) and the Office of the Under Secretary for Management play key roles in overseeing major acquisition programs like TECS Mod. For example, the CIO's responsibilities include setting departmental IT policies, processes, and standards; and ensuring that IT acquisitions comply with DHS IT management processes, technical requirements, and approved enterprise architecture, among other things. Within the Office of the CIO, the Enterprise Business Management Office has been given primary responsibility for ensuring that the department's IT investments align with its missions and objectives. As part of its responsibilities, this office periodically assesses IT investments to gauge how well they are performing through a review of program risk, human capital, cost and schedule, and requirements.

In October 2011, DHS's Under Secretary for Management established the Office of Program Accountability and Risk Management (PARM). The office is to ensure the effectiveness of the overall program execution governance process and has the responsibility for developing and maintaining DHS's Acquisition Management Directive.[6] It is also responsible for providing independent assessments of major investment

---

[6]The Acquisition Management Directive provides the overall policy and structure for acquisition management within the department and is used in planning and executing acquisitions.

programs—called a Quarterly Program Accountability Report, and identifying emerging risks and issues that DHS needs to address.

In December 2011, DHS introduced a new initiative to improve and streamline the department's IT program governance.[7] This initiative established a tiered governance structure for program execution. Among other things, this new structure includes a series of governance bodies, each chartered with specific decision responsibilities for each major investment. Among these are executive steering committees, which serve as the primary decision-making authorities for DHS's major acquisition programs. The steering committees, which are generally chaired by officials from the DHS agency responsible for the acquisition, are responsible for providing guidance to program management offices, approving program milestone documentation, and making important program execution decisions, as requested by the program manager and/or key stakeholders.

In September 2011, ICE chartered an executive steering committee responsible for overseeing its TECS modernization program. ICE's committee is chaired by the Deputy Associate Director of Homeland Security Investigations and includes voting representation from CBP, as well as other stakeholders. Members include DHS's CIO and Chief Financial Officer, stakeholder groups (such as U.S Citizenship and Immigration Services),[8] and CBP's TECS Mod Program Manager. The steering committee has been meeting since December 2011.

In early 2013, CBP developed an executive steering committee with responsibility for overseeing its TECS modernization effort.[9] It held its first governance meeting in February 2013 and is chaired by CBP's Assistant Commissioner, Office of Information and Technology, and Chief Information Officer/Lead Technical Authority. Members include DHS's Under Secretary for Science and Technology, CIO, and Chief Financial

---

[7]DHS, *Integrated Strategy for High Risk Management* (December 2011).

[8] U.S. Citizenship and Immigration Services (USCIS) administers immigration and naturalization adjudication functions and establishes immigration services policies and priorities.

[9]Prior to setting up this structure, TECS modernization was governed by an Integrated Governance Committee which met bimonthly between July 2011 and September 2012, and a joint executive steering committee which met semiannually between July 2011 and June 2012.

Officer; as well as representatives from stakeholder groups and ICE's TECS Mod Program Manager.

Figure 2 shows the relationships between the oversight and governance boards involved with the two programs.

Figure 2: Relationships between DHS Oversight and Governance Entities

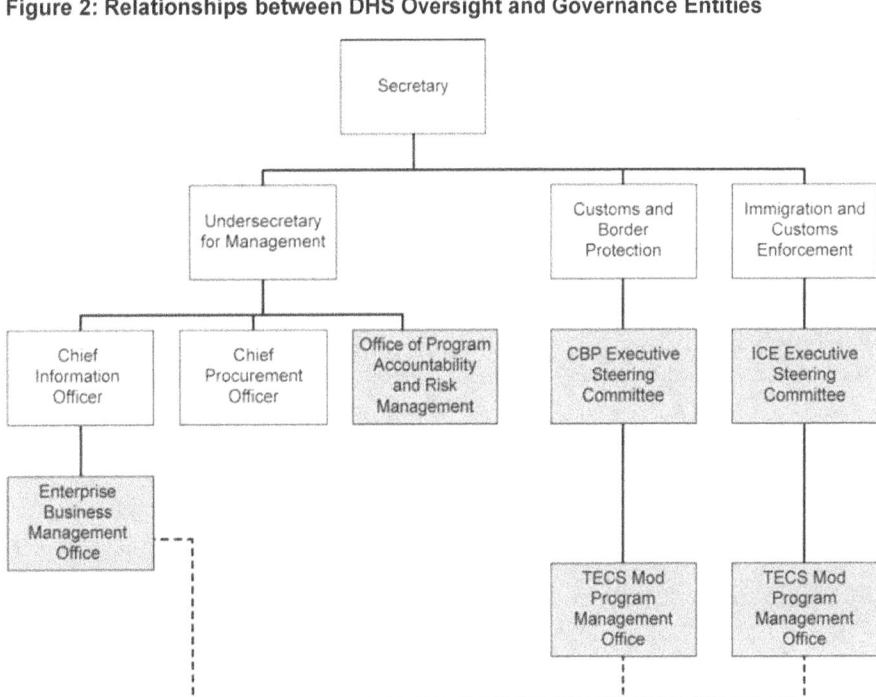

Source: GAO analysis of DHS data

GAO Previously Reported on DHS's Management of IT Investments, Including TECS Modernization

We have previously reported on DHS's management of its major investments generally, and the management and development of TECS modernization specifically. [10]

- In July 2012, we reported[11] that DHS had introduced a new IT governance framework that was generally consistent with recent Office of Management and Budget guidance and with best practices for managing projects and portfolios identified in our IT Investment Management framework. [12] Specifically, of the nine practices in the framework, we found that the department's new governance framework partially addressed two and fully addressed seven others. For example, consistent with Office of Management and Budget guidance calling for the CIO to play a significant role in overseeing programs, DHS's draft procedures required that lower-level boards overseeing IT programs include the DHS CIO, a component CIO, or a designated executive representative from a CIO office. In addition, consistent with practices identified in the framework, DHS's draft procedures identified key performance indicators for gauging portfolio performance. However, it had not completed its policies and procedures, because, according to department officials, the focus had been on piloting the new governance process. We recommended that DHS finalize associated policies and procedures, and fully follow best practices for implementing the process. DHS concurred with our recommendations.
- Regarding the performance of the TECS modernization effort, in a September 2012 report, [13] we noted that CBP's program encountered delays because program officials needed to develop new requirements to accommodate users' requests to interface with an

---

[10]GAO, *Information Technology: DHS Needs to Enhance Management of Cost and Schedule for Major Investments*, GAO-12-904 (Washington, D.C.: Sept. 26, 2012); *Department of Homeland Security: Continued Progress Made Improving and Integrating Management Areas, but More Work Remains*, GAO-12-1041T (Washington, D.C.: Sept. 20, 2012); *Homeland Security: DHS Requires More Disciplined Investment Management to Help Meet Mission Needs*, GAO-12-833 (Washington, D.C.: Sept. 18, 2012); *Information Technology: DHS Needs to Further Define and Implement Its New Governance Process*; GAO-12-818 (Washington, D.C.: July 25, 2012); and *Data Mining: DHS Needs to Improve Executive Oversight of Systems Supporting Counterterrorism*, GAO-11-742 (Washington, D.C.: Sept. 7, 2011).

[11]GAO-12-818.

[12]GAO-04-394G.

[13]GAO-12-904.

additional system. Additional delays were caused by questions about whether the system duplicated functions performed by another agency system. We recommended that DHS guidance address shortcomings and develop corrective actions for all major IT investment projects having cost and schedule shortfalls, including TECS Mod. DHS agreed with our recommendation.

- In September 2011,[14] we reported that CBP modernization program officials reported delays in completing required program documentation due, in part, to their not understanding the approval processes at the department level. We further noted that, although the program had recently been reviewed and approved by the DHS acquisition review board,[15] CBP's program office had not completed the required acquisition plan the board typically uses to evaluate system effectiveness and alignment with the agency's mission. In addition, the program had not yet completed privacy impact assessments that covered the entire program. We recommended that DHS address these shortfalls and the department concurred.

CBP TECS Modernization Scope Defined, Schedule and Cost of Both Modernization Programs Are Unclear

CBP has defined the scope for its modernization program, but its schedule and cost continue to change and are being revised. Further, ICE is overhauling the scope, schedule, and cost of its program after discovering that its initial solution is not technically viable. Thus, it is unclear whether these programs are on track to deliver planned functionality by September 2015.

---

[14]GAO-11-742.

[15]The acquisition review board reviews major acquisition programs at key milestones based, in part, on information provided by PARM, and decides whether a program will be authorized to proceed to the next life-cycle phase.

CBP Has Defined the Scope of Its TECS Modernization Program; but Schedule and Cost Commitments Are Uncertain

CBP has defined the scope of its program to include the replacement of its aging current mainframe-based platform with a mixture of hardware, and custom-developed and commercial software. Further, CBP plans to move data from the legacy TECS system to databases hosted at DHS's data centers and to use DHS's network infrastructure. CBP expects that its modernization efforts will yield certain improvements over the existing system, including the following.

- Enhancements to TECS' search algorithms to better match names from foreign alphabets; address gaps in current processes that could result in missing a person of interest. This includes an improved ability for inspectors to update information on travelers at air and sea borders at the time of encounter.
- Improvements in the flow and integration of data between CBP and its partner agencies and organizations. This is intended to aid the agency's inspectors by providing timely, complete, and accurate information about a traveler during the secondary inspection process.

CBP planned to develop, deploy, and implement these capabilities incrementally across five projects from 2008 to 2015.

- Secondary Inspection: This project is to support processing of travelers referred from primary inspection for either enforcement or administrative reasons. [16] According to CBP, this project's functionality was fully deployed to all air and sea ports of entry in 2011, and was fully deployed to all land ports of entry in 2013.
- High Performance Primary Query and Manifest Processing: This project is intended to improve TECS data search results in order to expedite the processing of manifests[17] from individuals traveling to the United States on commercial or private aircraft, and commercial vessels. It is to be fully operational by March 2015.
- Travel Document and Encounter Data: This project is intended to improve CBP's ability to query and validate travel documentation for

---

[16]The primary inspection process is the first part of the inspection process where CBP officers inspect travelers and their travel documents to determine if they may be admitted or should be referred for further questioning and document examination. If additional review is necessary, the traveler is referred to secondary inspection where another officer makes a final determination to admit or deny admission.

[17]A manifest is a list of passengers or an invoice of cargo for a vehicle or vessel (like a ship or plane).

both passengers and their means of conveyance. It is to be fully operational by March 2015.

- Lookout Record Data and Services: This project is intended to improve the efficiency of existing data screening and analyses capabilities. It is to be fully operational by March 2015.
- Primary Inspection Processes: This project is intended to modernize the overall inspection process and provide support for additional or random screening and communication functions. It is to be fully operational by March 2015.

As part of each of these projects, CBP is also developing an online access portal, called TECS Portal, for authorized users to access information remotely using a modern web- browser, along with security and infrastructure improvements, and the migration of data from the current system to databases in the new environment at the DHS datacenter. Ultimately, TECS Mod functionality is to be deployed to over 340 ports of entry across the United States.

To date, Secondary Inspection is operational approximately 6 months earlier than was estimated in the program's 2012 acquisition program baseline. In addition, CBP reports that a portion of the High Performance Primary Query and Manifest Processing project is also operational. The remaining projects are all scheduled to be operational by March 2015. Appendix IV provides additional information about these projects.

However, the program is revising its schedule and cost baselines, making its remaining commitments uncertain. Specifically, the program is revising its acquisition program baseline for a second time in under a year. In particular, CBP revised the program's initial acquisition program baseline in November 2012, establishing new commitments for the program's cost and schedule for each of the projects, as well as the program overall. According to program officials in June 2013, CBP is in the process of again revising its program baseline, and plans to do so by September 2013. Officials explained that this time, CBP is revising its commitments to reflect actual cost and schedule data gathered since its last revision.

The completion dates for each of CBP's five projects have changed over time. Specifically, four of the projects are scheduled to be delivered later than originally planned and one project—Primary Inspection Processes— is scheduled to be completed ahead of the initial schedule. For example, according to the October 2009 program plan, Secondary Inspection was to be operational in September 2012. That operational date was then modified in the program's acquisition program baseline (which was approved in October 2010) to be June 2013 (9 months later than originally scheduled). Then, in May 2011, CBP notified DHS that it was going to miss the deadline for several of its schedule milestones, including Secondary Inspection. [18] As a result, CBP revised its schedule baseline for TECS Mod in November 2012; the new operational date for the project was to be March 2014. That date was reiterated in the CBP-ICE Joint Integration Process document, signed by CBP and ICE program management, upon its release in April 2013. [19] However, shortly thereafter, the program again revised the operational date to be September 2013. Figure 3 illustrates the changes to CBP's schedules for the five projects over time.

Figure 3: Changes to CBP TECS Mod's Schedules for Full Operational Capability over Time, as Depicted in Various Program Documents

	2012	2013	2014	2015
	J F M A M J J A S O N D	J F M A M J J A S O N D	J F M A M J J A S O N D	J F M A M J J A S O N D
Secondary inspection				
High performance primary query				
Travel documents and encounter data				
Lookout record data and services				
Primary inspection processes				

○ October 2009 TECS Modernization Program Plan

◐ October 2010 Acquisition Program Baseline

◔ November 2012 Acquisition Program Baseline

● April 2013 TECS Modernization CBP – ICE Joint Integration Process Document

Source: GAO analysis of DHS data

---

[18] Six CBP TECS Mod key events had breached their scheduled thresholds by June 2011, including the TECS platform privacy impact assessment, awarding an application developer contract, the critical design review for the Secondary Inspection land project, and the production readiness review, initial operating capability and operational testing for the High Performance Primary Query project.

[19] The Joint Integration Process describes a series of actions and processes CBP and ICE will cooperatively undertake to modernize both agencies' portions of the existing TECS system, and includes a program schedule.

Exacerbating the rebaselining and the schedule changes over time is the fact that CBP has not fully developed its master schedule to manage work activities and to monitor the program's progress. Our research has identified, among other things, that a key element associated with a complete and useful schedule or roadmap for executing a program such as TECS Mod is to logically sequence all work activities so that start and finish dates of future activities, as well as key events based on the status of completed and in-progress activities, can be reliably forecast. [20] While the program office has developed high-level schedules for each of its projects, officials explained that the program has not fully defined and documented all the linkages between work activities within the individual project schedules, nor have they defined dependencies that exist between projects in the master schedule. The program's master schedule provided to us in May 2013 showed that approximately 65 percent of CBP's remaining work activities were not linked with other associated work activities. Without these linkages, activities that slip early in the schedule do not transmit delays to activities that should depend on them, and a critical path[21] cannot be determined, which means that management is unable to determine how a slip in the completion date of a particular task may affect the overall project schedule. Moreover, as of June 2013, the program had not yet developed a detailed schedule for the last project, Primary Inspection Processes, nor had it completed a detailed schedule for parts of the second project, High Performance Primary Query. Instead of managing from a fully developed master schedule, officials explained that they manage the program according to the milestones in the program's acquisition program baseline, and do so by sharing information about project and program dependencies at meetings between project teams. However, the lack of a complete schedule raises questions about the validity of the milestones in its acquisition program baseline, and the certainty of the program's schedule commitments.

Furthermore, the program's current schedule assumes the concurrent delivery of four of the five projects. As we have previously reported, the concurrent development of system components (e.g., the five TECS

---

[20]GAO, *GAO Schedule Assessment Guide: Best Practices for Project Schedules, Exposure Draft*, GAO-12-120G (Washington, D.C.: May 2012).

[21]The critical path represents the chain of dependent activities with the longest total duration in the schedule. If any activity in the critical path slips, the entire project will be delayed.

modernization projects) introduces risks that could adversely impact program cost and schedule.[22] Such risks include the contention for limited resources. For the CBP TECS modernization program, these risks may be realized. In particular, program officials told us that development work for the Primary Inspection Processes was halted because of anticipated funding shortfalls due to sequestration.[23] However, when the funding shortfalls were not realized, the program was unable to initiate Primary Inspection Processes development because, according to the Passenger Systems Program Office Executive Director, the program's contractor resources had been diverted to other projects and shifting those resources back to Primary Inspection Processes would affect work on these projects. The Executive Director further stated that if work on Primary Inspection did not begin by January 2014, the program would not meet its operational date of September 2015.

Program officials said that reasons for the schedule weaknesses include a lack of appropriate and skilled resources. Specifically, program officials stated that the program has only two staff members with skills needed to develop and maintain the schedules, and that fully documenting all the dependencies would be time consuming and not worth the effort because in their view, the limitations in the integrated master schedule were not sufficient to warrant the additional resources that would be necessary to fix them. However, without a complete and integrated master schedule that includes all program work activities and associated dependencies, CBP is not in a position to accurately determine the amount of time required to complete its TECS modernization effort and develop realistic milestones. Moreover, the program does not have a basis for guiding the projects' execution and measuring progress, thus increasing the agency's risk of not meeting the program's completion dates.

Similar to TECS Mod's schedule milestones, the program's cost estimates have also changed as a result of rebaselining, and are currently being revised. The program's current baselined life-cycle cost estimate[24]

---

[22] See for example, GAO, *Information Technology: Customs Has Made Progress on Automated Commercial Environment System, but It Faces Long-Standing Management Challenges and New Risks*, GAO-06-580 (Washington, D.C.: May 2006).

[23] The Budget Control Act of 2011 (Pub. L. No. 112-25, Aug. 2, 2011) called for across-the-board budget reductions (i.e., sequestration) in federal government programs for fiscal years 2013 through 2021.

[24] This estimate is in the program's November 2012 acquisition program baseline.

is approximately $724 million, including $31 million for planning management, $212 million for development, and $481 million for operations and maintenance. However, as previously stated, the program is in the process of revising its estimate. As of August 2013, the program reported that it had expended about $226 million—approximately $170 million for planning/program management and development/acquisition, and $56 million for operations and maintenance.

While officials reaffirmed their intention to complete the whole program by the 2015 deadline, the program faces the risk of not doing so because its specific schedule milestones for each of the projects are based on incomplete schedule information and concurrency among the projects has resulted in competition for the same contracting resources. Moreover, while the program is pending rebaselining, it is unclear when the program actually intends to deliver functionality, or how much it will cost to do so.

ICE Established TECS Modernization's Scope, Schedule, and Costs, but Technical Issues Have Caused ICE to Overhaul Its Design and Commitments

ICE initially defined the scope of its TECS modernization effort to include specific law enforcement and criminal justice information functions; tools to support ICE officers' collection of information, data analysis, and management operations; enhanced capabilities to access and create data linkages with information resources from elsewhere in DHS and other law enforcement agencies; and capabilities to better enable investigative and intelligence operations, corresponding management activities, and information sharing. Further, ICE established plans to deliver functionality in two phases, Core Case Management and Comprehensive Case Management, each of which was to contain several releases. Specifically:

- Phase 1: Core Case Management: This phase was to encompass all case management functions currently included in the existing system. ICE planned to develop and deploy these functions in three releases beginning in 2009, and was scheduled to deploy Release 1 by December 2013, with additional releases following about every 12 months, in order to achieve independence from the existing TECS platform by September 2015. Specific capabilities that were to be provided include:

  - basic electronic case management functions, including opening cases, performing supervisory review of cases, and closing cases within the system;
  - development of reports for use as evidentiary material in court proceedings arising from ICE agents' investigations;
  - maintenance of records relating to the subjects of ICE investigations; and

- audit capabilities to monitor system usage.

- Phase 2: Comprehensive Case Management: This phase was to expand on the features delivered as part of phase one and to be delivered in four increments starting in 2016, with an estimated completion date in fiscal year 2017.

Regarding costs, ICE's baselined life-cycle cost estimate[25] is approximately $818 million, including about $17 million for planning, roughly $328 million for development and acquisition, and approximately $473 million for operations and maintenance.

However, in 2012 the program began to experience technical issues, which resulted in a delay of approximately 7 months and the deferral or removal of functionality from Release 1. Specifically, ICE decided in 2012 that Release 1 would only provide functionality for the "person" type of subject records; all the other types of subject records have been deferred to future releases. [26] Then, in October 2012, the agency conducted a review of the program's remaining work for Release 1 to determine whether, in light of increasing rates of program defects and a slowdown in the program's overall progress, ICE was positioned to deliver Release 1 as planned. Based on the review results, the agency deferred or eliminated approximately 3,000 out of the 4,300 in-scope requirements (about 70 percent of the original total) in order for the program to meet its planned schedule commitments. Such functionality includes the capability to perform supervisory review of cases and certain electronic notifications and alerts.

Faced with continuing technical issues and related delays, ICE's program manager said that the program initiated a second program review in January 2013 at the direction of its executive steering committee and with participation from the program office, the contractor, and Homeland Security Investigations. Based on the review results, the program office determined in June 2013 that the system under development was not technically viable and would not be fielded as part of ICE's final solution due to ongoing technical difficulties relative to the user interface, access controls, and case-related data management. Instead of continuing with the current technical solution, the program manager explained that, after

---

[25]This estimate is in the program's May 2011 acquisition program baseline.

[26]Other types of subject records include "business" and "vehicle," among others.

having spent approximately $19 million in acquisition/development costs on the original solution, the program would seek alternatives and start over. The program manager said ICE is now assessing such alternatives, including a revised technical approach offered by the current development contractor, as well as other off-the-shelf solutions in use at other agencies. According to the program manager, significant portions of the previous solution's data migration and infrastructure-related components might be salvaged for reuse in whatever new solution is chosen. But, depending on the approach selected, most of the user interfaces, security components, and business rules that have been developed for the program to date are unlikely to be reused.

The program manager stated that the program intends to decide which course it will pursue by October 2013, and based on that decision, it will update the program's life-cycle cost estimate, schedule, and requirements documents (as needed). Further, he stated that ICE intends to proactively revise its May 2011 acquisition program baseline before it breaches at the end of December 2013 and reaffirmed the agency's intention to deploy a solution by the 2015 deadline. In the meantime, according to the program manager, ICE has largely halted development work and it will be January 2014 at the earliest before any new development work begins. Given the time lost in developing the current technical solution, as well as the already reduced program scope, ICE cannot say what specific features it will release to users, what its schedule for deploying this functionality will be, or how much such efforts will cost. Without clearly defining these commitments, ICE is at risk of not achieving independence from the existing system by 2015.

TECS Modernization's Risk Management Is Generally Consistent with Leading Practices, but Requirements Management Has Had Mixed Results

Both agencies have generally implemented risk management practices, but they have had mixed results in managing requirements for their programs. While they have managed many of the risks in accordance with recognized leading practices, neither agency has identified all known risks and escalated them for timely review by senior management. Further, while CBP's requirements management processes and practices are largely consistent with leading practices, key requirements activities were well underway before such practices were established. In addition, ICE was operating without documented requirements management guidance for several years, and its requirements development and management activities were mismanaged as a result. ICE has recently developed guidance that is consistent with leading practices, but has not yet implemented it.

CBP and ICE Have Generally Implemented Risk Management Practices

Risk management is a process for anticipating problems and taking appropriate steps to mitigate risks and minimize their impact on project commitments. According to relevant guidance,[27] effective risk management practices include, among other things:

- establishing and documenting risk management strategies;
- assigning roles and responsibilities for managing risks;
- creating a risk inventory, documenting all risks in it, prioritizing them, and developing plans to mitigate them; and
- regularly tracking the status of risks and mitigation efforts, including the documentation of triggers to escalate risks for review by senior management.

CBP Has Developed a Risk Strategy and Inventory, but Has Not Identified or Escalated All Known Risks

Of the four leading practices, CBP fully implemented two practices and partially implemented two practices (see table 1). Specifically, it has documented a risk management strategy and established roles and responsibilities for managing risks. However, while the agency established a risk inventory, it has not identified all of the risks facing the program. In addition, CBP only partially implemented tracking of risks because it did not define thresholds for risks that would trigger the automatic review by senior management and thus did not always escalate risks to senior management's attention, and because it does not identify all information necessary for tracking risks.

---

[27]*CMMI for Development*, version 1.3.

Table 1: CBP Implementation of Leading Risk Management Practices

Leading practice	Status	CBP processes
Establishing and documenting a risk management strategy	●	CBP established and documented a risk management strategy that includes processes for identifying, categorizing, analyzing, and prioritizing risks. For example, the strategy outlines possible sources of risks, including a review of the project scope and budget, generic risk identification checklists and techniques, and project-specific risk suggestions gathered from meeting discussions and e-mails.
Assigning roles and responsibilities for managing risks	●	CBP established roles and responsbilities for risk management. Each project has a Project Risk Manager responsible for verifying that risks are identified, documented, analyzed, and tracked. The Project Risk Managers also review the risks for updates and run various reports to track project risks. The TECS Mod Program Risk Manager is responsble for ensuring that the program has a risk management strategy, that project members are aware of it and kept up to date on any changes to it, and that risk assessments are conducted as described by the strategy. Further, the manager ensures that risks are discussed at weekly project meetings and also facilities the twice-monthly meetings of the TECs Mod Risk Review Board. The board meetings are attended by the Program Manager and/or Executive Director, and other staff relevant to the risk process. At the meetings, the board reviews ongoing risks, develops and reviews risk mitigation plans, and assigns action items to implement the mitigation plans.
Creating a risk inventory, documenting all risks in it, prioritizing them, and developing plans for their mitigation	◐	CBP created a risk inventory that contains risks, their prioritization, and mitigation plans; however, CBP did not document and manage all known risks. Specifically, long-standing problems, including the lack of a quality integrated master schedule (as discussed earlier in this report), and the absence of an earned value management tool,[a] (as discussed later in this report) were not documented as formal risks.
Regularly tracking the status of risks and mitigation efforts, including the documentation of triggers to escalate risks for review by senior management	◐	CBP tracks the status of risks and mitigation efforts in the risk inventory. However, neither the risk strategy nor the risk inventory includes thresholds for cost, schedule, or performance problems which, if exceeded, would trigger automatic review of the risk by senior management. Instead, decisions on when to escalate risks for executive review outside of the program are made by the TECS Mod Program Manager based on her understanding of the magnitude and complexity of such risks and her ability and scope of authority to address the problems. However, without documented triggers or thresholds for elevating risks, some may be missed. For example, a problem regarding lack of sufficient contractor staff for system design development and testing activities was identified in January 2012, but was not escalated for review until the April 2013 Executive Steering Committee meeting. In addition, the inventory does not identify the date when each risk was last reviewed. CBP officials also noted that each risk is reviewed at least biweekly, but other than updating the date of the entire risk inventory, there is no information on when an individual risk was last updated.

Key:

● – The practice was fully implemented.
◐ – The practice was partially implemented.
○ – The practice was not implemented.

Source: GAO analysis of CBP data.

[a]Earned value management is a process for measuring a project's progress by comparing the value of work accomplished with the amount of work expected to be completed, and is based on variances from cost and schedule baselines. The industry standard is found in ANSI/EIA 748-B, Earned Value Management Systems, approved July 2007.

Reasons why concerns we identified were not documented as risks, include the program office officials' view that the limitations in the integrated master schedule were not sufficient to warrant the additional resources that would be necessary to fix them, and that the lack of a fully defined schedule was not a program risk, as well as the existing contractor's lack of skills and capability to implement earned value management. However, both an integrated master schedule and earned value management are important tools for effective program management and oversight, and the absence of such capabilities increases the risk that a program like TECS will not deliver its intended capabilities within cost and schedule commitment. Therefore, until all of the risks have been captured in the risk inventory with the necessary information to track the status, thresholds have been defined to trigger review by senior management, and relevant risks have been escalated to senior management in a timely manner, key decision makers will be less than fully informed. Further, the program will likely continue to experience the types of problems discussed earlier in this report.

ICE Has Developed a Risk Strategy and Inventory, but Has Not Identified All Known Risks

ICE fully implemented two of the leading risk management practices and partially implemented two others (see table 2). Specifically, it defined and documented a risk management strategy, and established roles and responsibilities for risk identification, tracking, and monitoring. The program office has also established a risk inventory with mitigation plans, but it has not identified all of the known risks. Further, while ICE has tracked the status of risks and mitigation efforts, it has not always followed its own processes for escalating risks outside of the program for senior management's attention.

Table 2: ICE Implementation of Leading Risk Management Practices

Leading practice	Status	ICE processes
Establishing and documenting a risk management strategy	●	ICE established and documented a risk management strategy which includes processes for identifying, categorizing, analyzing, and prioritizing risks. For example, the strategy identifies sources of possible risks, including comparisons with similar processes, relevant lessons learned studies, and results from tests and prototype development.
Assigning roles and responsibilities for managing risks	●	ICE established roles and responsibilities for risk management. The Risk Management Coordinator is responsble for updating and maintaining the risk inventory on a weekly basis. The Risk Management Coordinator also works with the Program Manager, the Program Management Office, and the project leads to develop risk reports for review at senior management level meetings, which are held bimonthly and monthly.
Creating a risk inventory, documenting all risks in it, prioritizing them, and developing plans for their mitigation	◑	ICE created a risk inventory that contains risks, their prioritization, and mitigation plans; however, it did not document and manage all known risks. For example, program officials stated that in October 2012 they identified problems with the backlog of requirements for Release 1, and in January 2013 they identified concerns that the technical solution proposed by the development contractor might not be technologically sufficient to support the core case management functionality—both which would therefore jeopardize the schedule for delivery of Release 1. However, those risks were not entered into the inventory until March and April 2013. In addition, although at one time the risk inventory contained a risk related to requirements management concerns—such as developing requirements without a documented requirements management strategy—this risk was closed after initial steps had been taken to address the concerns. According to the program manager, it turned out that the requirements management activities were not being effectively implemented, but the program was not aware until problems were revealed by the results of integrated testing of Release 1 in fall 2012.
Regularly tracking the status of risks and mitigation efforts, including the documentation of triggers to escalate risks for review by senior management	◑	ICE tracks the status of risks and mitigation efforts, but has not identified thresholds that trigger the escalation of risks for management attention. Although the inventory contains fields for the identification of threshold dates and events for risks to be escalated to management for review, program officials told us in May 2013 that the program had discontinued the use of these fields. In July 2013, officials stated that they were reevaluating the data elements in the risk inventory and would consider adding threshold dates and events back into the risk inventory.

Key:
● – The practice was fully implemented.
◑ – The practice was partially implemented.
○ – The practice was not implemented.

Source: GAO analysis of ICE data.

According to ICE officials, they did not document the problems with the requirements backlog and technical solution in the program's risk inventory because they did not want to make the risks visible until they understood the full extent of their scope, and they only included the risks in the inventory after attempts to address the problem failed. However, key to effective risk management is early identification of risks, so that they are known and visible as early as possible in order to manage and mitigate them, and ultimately, minimize impact to the program. Until all risks are captured in the risk inventory, thresholds are defined, and risks are shared with senior management in a timely manner, the program may continue to experience additional requirements and technical problems discussed earlier in this report.

CBP and ICE Requirements Management Processes and Practices Are Largely Consistent with Leading Practices, but Were Established after Requirements Activities Were Underway

Well-defined and managed requirements are a cornerstone of effective system development and acquisition efforts. According to recognized guidance,[28] a documented and disciplined process for developing and managing requirements can help reduce the risk of developing a system that does not meet user needs, cannot be adequately tested, and does not perform or function as intended. Such a process includes, among other things,

- establishing a process for developing and managing requirements to ensure that requirements are identified, reviewed, and controlled;
- assigning and defining the roles and responsibilities for all those involved in requirements management activities;
- eliciting user needs, translating them into requirements, and analyzing them to ensure that each requirement is unique, unambiguous, and testable; and
- defining a disciplined change control process.

CBP's Requirements Management Is Largely Consistent with Leading Practices, but Developed after Key Requirements Activities Were Performed

Of the four practices for requirements management, CBP fully implemented three and partially implemented one other (see table 3). Specifically, it established a requirements management process, assigned roles and responsibilities for requirements development and management activities, and defined a change control process. However, although CBP elicited user needs and translated them into requirements, CBP could not document how and if each requirement was analyzed to ensure that it is unique, unambiguous, and testable.

---

[28]*CMMI for Development*, version 1.3.

Table 3: CBP Implementation of Leading Requirements Management Practices

Leading practice	Status	CBP processes
Establishing a process for developing and managing requirements to ensure that requirements are identified, reviewed, and controlled	●	CBP established a requirements management process which describes the activities to identify, collect, review, monitor, and control requirements. For example, the plan discusses requirements management concepts including the various types and levels of requirements (e.g., operational, functional, and technical), and the mandatory and optional attributes (e.g., source/origin, date certified, status) that are used to clarify each individual requirement.
Assigning and defining the roles and responsibilities for all those involved in requirements management activities	●	CBP established roles and responsibilities for requirements management. Specifically, each of the projects has a Requirements Analyst who is responsible for leading the requirements elicitation, definition, and baseline management. The Requirements Analysts are overseen by the Program Requirements Manager, who coordinates the day-to-day requirements development and management activities for the program. A Business Requirements Management Board, which includes branch directors, provides governance and oversight.
Eliciting user needs, translating them into requirements, and analyzing them to ensure that each requirement is unique, unambiguous, and testable	◑	CBP elicited user needs and translated them into requirements, which have been reviewed and certified. However, it is unknown whether CBP fully analyzed each requirement. For example, CBP initially elicited user needs during meetings held with internal users from CBP and other DHS agencies such as ICE and the U.S. Coast Guard, as well as external users from other departments including the Departments of Agriculture, Justice, Labor, State, and Treasury. At these meetings, stakeholders reviewed existing system documentation and legacy software code, and used these as the basis for the TECS modernization requirements. As part of this exercise, users were tasked with determining whether existing system functionality was appropriate and needed in the modernized system, or whether changes needed to be made. The resulting requirements were then reviewed during a peer review process by project stakeholders, project leaders from other projects, and the Systems Engineering Integrated Product Team. Finally, the requirements were certified by the Office of Field Operations, who is the project's business owner. However, there is no evidence that requirements were analyzed to ensure that each was unique, unambiguous, and testable. CBP officials told us they analyzed the requirements during the peer review process; however, the description of how to do so is not defined in the requirements management process and CBP could not provide documentation or results to show that this analysis was performed during the peer review.
Defining a disciplined change control process	●	CBP has a defined change control process. CBP uses the Passenger Systems Program Office *Change Management Process and Procedure* to guide its change control processes for the modernized TECS software. The procedure documents the steps to be taken for changes to certified functional requirements, beginning with the submission to the team lead of a standardized form requesting the change.

Key:
● – The practice was fully implemented.
◑ – The practice was partially implemented.
○ – The practice was not implemented.
Source: GAO analysis of CBP data.

Although CBP's current requirements process largely addresses the leading practices, it was not established until March 2012, and so therefore was not used to guide requirements development for the majority of the program. Specifically, prior to March 2012, the program used the Passenger Systems Program Office requirements guidance for requirements elicitation and documentation, which, according to officials, was too generic to meet the needs of the program. In particular, the guidance allowed each of the projects to develop requirements independently of each other, and document them without standardization. According to CBP officials, the requirements for the projects that were developed earlier in the program—such as Secondary Inspection and High Performance Primary Query—were not as consistently well-formed or detailed as subsequent projects because of the lack of a rigorous process. Without well-defined and implemented processes for analyzing requirements to ensure that they are unique, unambiguous, and testable, CBP risks TECS Mod not performing as intended in the users' environments, or taking longer to develop and test.

ICE Mismanaged Requirements in the Past, but Recently Issued a Process to Improve Its Management Moving Forward

For several years, ICE operated without an established requirements management process, which resulted in significant problems for the program. Although the agency began development of requirements in June 2009, the program did not have a documented requirements management process in place to guide its activities until March 2011, when ICE issued a requirements management process that reflected the program's initial intent to use a traditional system development approach. However, that process became outdated a few months later in October 2011 when the program transitioned to an Agile development methodology.[29] Rather than refine or replace its newly-issued requirements management process, officials proceeded without one until the current requirements management documents were issued in March 2013. As shown in table 4, ICE's requirements development and management activities during this time only partially satisfied one of the four leading practices, and did not satisfy the other three.

---

[29]Agile software development calls for the delivery of software in small, short increments rather than in the typically long, sequential phases of a traditional software development approach. Agile emphasizes early and continuous software delivery, as well as using collaborative teams, and measuring progress with working software.

Table 4: ICE Implementation of Leading Requirements Management Practices

Leading practice	Status	ICE documents
Establishing a process for developing and managing requirements to ensure that requirements are identified, reviewed, and controlled	○	ICE operated without a documented requirements management process during most of the program development. Initially, the program operated without an established process from June 2009 to early 2011, when the bulk of the original requirements were developed. While ICE established a requirements process using a traditional methodology approach in early 2011, this became outdated in October 2011, when the program transitioned to an Agile approach.
Assigning and defining the roles and responsibilities for all those involved in requirements management activities	○	Without a documented process, roles and responsibilities for requirements management activities were unclear. According to program officials, government and contractor staff have had a hard time coming up to speed on Agile requirements management concepts and had to have refresher training as recently as February 2013.
Eliciting user needs, translating them into requirements, and analyzing them to ensure that each requirement is unique, unambiguous, and testable	◐	ICE elicited user needs from June 2009 to October 2009 and from January 2011 to March 2011. These needs were translated into requirements. However, recent evidence shows that the analysis of these requirements was insufficient. Specifically, for the past several months—as part of the refocus effort—the agency has been revalidating the requirements which were elicited in 2009 and 2011 for clarity, testability, and applicability to the current design. As a result of this revalidation effort, in May 2013 the program identified 625 requirements that were excessive or obsolete and has deleted them, which is about 15 percent of the 4,268 total original requirements. In addition, ICE discovered that another 2,358 of the original requirements were not necessary for transitioning TECS Mod off of the mainframe, and so has deferred these requirements to later releases. Taken together, the 2,983 deleted and deferred requirements represent about 70 percent of the total original requirements.
Defining a disciplined change control process	○	ICE operated without a documented change control process for most of the TECS Mod development. A change control standard operating procedure was not issued until March 2013.

Key:
● – The practice was fully implemented.
◐ – The practice was partially implemented.
○ – The practice was not implemented.
Source: GAO analysis of ICE data.

As a result of these limitations, program officials told us that they and their contractor did not complete work on over 2,500 requirements that were necessary for Release 1 to function properly. This lapse was not identified until fall 2012, when system prototypes, which had previously passed individual component tests, were combined and then tested in an end-to-end manner for the first time in ICE's integrated test environment. According to ICE's Program Manager, the system failed such testing because of the unaccounted-for requirements. Analysis performed by the program revealed that it would take an additional 10 months of work to address the missing requirements. In order to meet its schedule commitments, ICE decided to eliminate or defer about 70 percent of the original requirements for Release 1. This in turn has contributed to the difficulties the agency faces in delivering the entire modernized system before the 2015 deadline.

In March 2013, ICE documented a new requirements management process for the Agile software development methodology it had adopted, and further established a change control board and standard operating procedure for managing changes to program requirements. Collectively, these two documents address all four of the leading practices called for in guidance as described below.

- ICE has defined a requirements management process that describes the practices to ensure requirements are elicited, reviewed, approved, and documented. For example, it describes the structure and tools to be used to organize and maintain the various types of requirements.
- The requirements management process identifies roles and responsibilities for requirements management. Specifically, the Requirements Manager, among other things, plans requirements management activities throughout the project development life cycle and maintains the requirements management strategy. The requirements analysts, among other things, participate in the elicitation, analysis, and refinement of program requirements. The requirements leads represent the needs of the product owner and the delivery team, and provide input on the prioritization of requirements.
- The requirements management process describes how user needs are to be collected and translated into requirements. The process also describes the attributes of a good requirement, including that it should be, among other things: (1) necessary—unique and not redundant to another requirement; (2) clear—not possible to interpret in more than one way and not in conflict with or contradictory to another requirement; and (3) verifiable—can be tested to determine whether or not the requirements is met.
- ICE has a defined change control process. Specifically, its new change control board standard operating procedure describes a process to ensure that (1) the process for system change requests is standardized, (2) system change requests are routed to appropriate staff for approval, (3) system change requests are processed in a timely manner, and (4) system change requests can be tracked.

These requirements management processes are essential to ensure that the TECS Mod system meets mission needs, performs as intended, and avoids the additional costly and time-consuming rework that the program has recently experienced.

DHS's Governance Bodies Have Taken Actions Aligned with Leading Practices, but Incomplete and Inaccurate Data Have Limited Their Effectiveness

Leading practices that we and others have identified[30] note that oversight is a critical element of an investment's life cycle, and that to be effective, oversight and governance bodies should, among other things,

- monitor a project's performance and progress toward predefined cost and schedule expectations;
- ensure that corrective actions are identified and assigned to the appropriate parties at the first sign of cost, schedule, and/or performance problems;
- ensure that these corrective actions are tracked until the desired outcomes are achieved; and
- rely on complete and accurate data to review the performance of IT projects and systems against stated expectations, including comparing estimated schedule time frames to actual schedule (including schedule slippages and/or compressions) and comparing estimated costs with funds spent or obligated to date, any changes in funding, and the impact of these changes.

As previously mentioned, DHS IT investments such as the two TECS modernization programs are overseen by governance bodies at multiple levels across DHS, including each programs' Executive Steering Committees and DHS's Office of the CIO. While the programs' steering committees have the authority to oversee all aspects of the execution of the programs between gates,[31] the Office of the CIO provides department-level oversight.

To their credit, these governance bodies have taken actions to address three of the four leading practices. Specifically,

- CBP's steering committee implemented two practices, although it is too soon to determine whether it has effectively implemented one of the other two practices;

- ICE's steering committee implemented three practices; and

the Office of the CIO implemented three practices.

---

[30]See *CMMI for Development*, version 1.3 and GAO-04-394G.

[31]DHS's Acquisition Life Cycle Framework defines key events called gates, where the Acquisition Review Board makes decisions regarding the investment's acquisition.

Table 5 shows whether or not each of the three governance bodies met the leading practices for performing oversight.

Table 5: Status of Whether DHS's TECS Mod Governance Bodies Met Leading Practices for Oversight

Leading practice	CBP Executive Steering Committee	ICE Executive Steering Committee	Office of the CIO
Monitor project's performance and progress toward predefined cost and schedule	Yes	Yes	Yes
Ensure that corrective actions are identified and assigned to the appropriate parties at the first sign of cost, schedule, and/or performance problems	Yes	Yes	Yes[a]
Ensure that corrective actions are tracked until the desired outcomes are achieved	n/a[b]	Yes	Yes[a]
Rely on complete and accurate data to review the performance of IT projects and systems against stated expectations	No	No	No

Source: GAO analysis of agency data.

Notes:

[a]This office implements this practice through its TechStat process, a face-to-face, evidence-based accountability review of an IT investment that enables the department to intervene to turn around, halt, or terminate projects that are failing or are not producing results. According to DHS's TechStat guide, an investment will be selected based on, among other criteria, its IT Dashboard rating—high-risk investments first, followed by high-impact medium-risk investments. Neither TECS Mod program has been a subject of a TechStat.

[b]Given that the steering committee has held only three meetings as of June 2013, it is too soon to tell whether it is effectively tracking corrective actions.

As shown in the table, the governance bodies implemented three of the four leading practices:

- **CBP Executive Steering Committee**. This body has implemented two leading practices: it monitors the program's performance and ensures corrective actions are identified. Specifically, it was chartered earlier this year and, as of June 2013, it has met three times since its formation.[32] In these meetings, the committee reviewed the program's cost and schedule performance, and assigned related action items to the appropriate individuals for closure. For example, during the February 2013 meeting, the committee discussed risks that could affect the program's cost and schedule, and created an action item for the program manager to discuss risk mitigation strategies with the Component Acquisition Executive.[33] The CBP Performance Manager stated that this action item was completed as of July 2013. In addition, the steering committee tracked action items from its initial meetings, but since there have only been three meetings as of June 2013, it is too soon to determine whether the committee is doing so consistently.

- **ICE Executive Steering Committee**. This body has implemented three leading practices: it monitors the program's performance, ensures corrective actions are identified, and generally tracks the action items to completion. For example, it discussed the program's cost and schedule performance in eight of the nine meetings since its inception in September 2011, has directed that actions be taken to address known issues, and generally tracked the action items to completion. Specifically, in a February 2013 meeting, the committee discussed schedule slippage and issues with cost estimates, and created an action item for the program to provide the committee estimated start and completion dates for a new life-cycle cost estimate. This action item was confirmed as "in progress" at the April 2013 meeting.
- **The Office of the CIO**. This office implemented three of the leading practices. Specifically, regarding monitoring, its Enterprise Business Management Office performs program health assessments to monitor an IT program's performance through a review of program risk, human capital, cost and schedule, contract oversight, and requirements. The assessment results in a weighted score between 1 and 100 that is then converted to the five-level CIO risk rating

---

[32]As previously stated, prior to the current governance structure, the programs were governed by an Integrated Governance Committee from July 2011 through September 2012, as well as a joint Executive Steering Committee that last met in June 2012. These governance bodies did not consistently perform a full review of both programs' cost, schedule, or risks, or assign and follow up on action items. ICE's current governance structure was established as part of the effort to test DHS's new governance framework; CBP's current governance structure was put into place as part of DHS's new governance structure.

[33] The Component Acquisition Executive is the senior acquisition official within the component responsible for management and oversight of the component's acquisition processes.

published on the Office of Management and Budget's IT Dashboard. [34] The frequency at which the office performs these assessments is based on each program's CIO rating of high, medium, or low risk. For example, it reviews high-risk programs monthly, medium-risk programs at least quarterly, and low-risk programs on a semiannual basis. When rating the TECS Mod programs, the Office of the CIO rated ICE's program as medium risk in March 2013 and CBP's program as moderately low risk in January 2013, which are the most recent ratings, as of July 2013.

The Office of the CIO identifies corrective actions during the program health assessments and ensures the actions are tracked to closure through its TechStat review process. [35] The CIO rating is used as one criterion to determine whether the program will be subject to a review. Any program that receives a high-risk rating is a candidate for a TechStat. As part of this process, the office assigns and follows up on corrective actions. However, neither program has been the subject of a TechStat because, as of July 2013, neither program was considered high risk.

In addition, PARM monitors the performance of major acquisition programs across DHS in order to identify any emerging risks and issues (such as cost and schedule problems), and then provides data to decision makers. In doing so, the office assesses programs against 15 separate criteria, similar to what is assessed in the program health assessment, including risk and requirements management, and cost and schedule performance, and creates a Quarterly Program Accountability Report. The report describes programs' value-to-risk ratio and, according to an agency official, is used as a tool to assess program risks and issues. PARM has created three of these reports thus far, but comparing the reports is difficult as the office changed the criteria and methodology to incorporate lessons learned. In the report for the third and fourth quarter

---

[34]See www.itdashboard.gov. This website, run by the Office of Management and Budget (OMB), displays federal agencies' cost, schedule, and performance data for over 700 major federal IT investments at 27 federal agencies that are responsible for about $40 billion of the federal budget. According to OMB, these data are intended to provide a near-real-time perspective on the performance of these investments, as well as a historical perspective.

[35]A TechStat is a face-to-face, evidence-based accountability review of an IT investment initiated by OMB that enables the department to intervene to turn around, halt, or terminate projects that are failing or are not producing results.

of fiscal year 2012,[36] the office rated both programs as high value, low risk.

However, while the governance bodies had taken actions to oversee the TECS modernization programs, the lack of complete, timely, and accurate data have affected their ability to make informed and timely decisions, thus limiting their effectiveness in several cases. For example:

- **Steering committees**. In an April 2013 meeting, the CBP program manager briefed the steering committee on its target milestone dates; even though the agency told us a month later that it had not fully defined its schedule, raising questions about the completeness and accuracy of the proposed milestone dates upon which the committee bases its oversight decisions. Similarly, in a February 2013 ICE steering committee meeting, the office of the CIO noted that the agency's program-provided life-cycle cost estimate was out of date and that a new one was needed before the program's cost and schedule performance could be measured accurately.

- **The Office of the CIO**. In its most recent program health assessments, the Enterprise Business Management Office partially based its rating of moderately low risk on CBP's use of earned value management; however, the program manager stated to us that the CBP program is not utilizing earned value management because neither they nor their development contractor had the capability to do so. Similarly, even though ICE had not reported recent cost or schedule data for its program—an issue that may signal a significant problem—OCIO rated ICE's program as medium risk. The reliance on incomplete and inaccurate date raises questions about the validity of the risk ratings.

- **PARM**. In the most recent Quarterly Program Accountability Report issued in early July 2013, PARM rated programs both as high value with low risk. However, CBP's low-risk rating is based in part on the program's master schedule and acquisition program baseline; however, as we stated earlier, problems with the agency's schedule raise questions about the validity and quality of those milestones. Further, the low-risk rating it issued for ICE is based, in part, on PARM's Quarterly Program Accountability Report for April through

---

[36]This report covers the time period from April to September 2012.

September 2012, which rated the program's cost performance with the lowest possible risk score. Yet, during that same time period, program documents show that cost and schedule performance was declining and varied significantly from its baseline. According to program documents, as of June 2012, TECS Mod had variances of 20 percent from its cost baseline and 13 percent from its schedule baseline. Moreover, both the cost and schedule estimates underlying the baseline were outdated.

Further, the Quarterly Program Accountability Report is not issued by PARM in a timely basis, and as such, it is not an effective tool for decision-makers. For example, the most recent report was published on July 7, 2013, over 9 months after the reporting period ended. Since then, ICE has experienced the issues with its technical solution described earlier in this report; and, as discussed, these issues have caused the program to halt development and replan its entire acquisition. As a result, the newly-issued issued report is not reflective of ICE's current status, and thus is not an effective tool for management's use.

Until these governance bodies base their reviews of performance on timely, complete, and accurate data, they will be limited in their ability to effectively provide oversight and to make timely decisions.

Conclusions

After spending millions of dollars and over 4 years on TECS modernization, it is unclear when it will be delivered and at what cost. While CBP's program has partially delivered one of the five major projects that comprise the program, program commitments are currently being revised, project milestones have changed over time, and the master schedule used by the program to manage its work activities and monitor progress has not been fully developed. These limitations raise doubts about the validity of the program's schedule commitments and greatly impact the program's ability to monitor and effectively manage its progress. A complete and integrated schedule provides the basis for valid schedule commitments; therefore it is important that as CBP revises its commitments, it ensure that its master schedule accurately reflects the work to be done, as well as the timing, sequencing, and dependencies between them. Moreover, ICE's program has made little progress in deploying its modernized case management system, and is now completely overhauling its original design and program commitments, placing the program in serious jeopardy of both not meeting the 2015 deadline and delaying the deployment of needed functionality. It is therefore imperative that the agency quickly develop and execute its revised strategy for implementing TECS Mod—including the functionality to be delivered, when it will be delivered, and how much it will cost.

Further, while both agencies have defined key practices for managing risks and requirements, the programs were not actively managing all risks and key requirements practices were developed after several key activities were performed. ICE in particular operated for years without a requirements management process, which resulted in poorly defined and incomplete requirements, and ultimately in costly rework and delays. Therefore, going forward, it is important that the programs implement these critical practices to help ensure that the program delivers the functionally needed to meet mission requirements and minimizes the potential for additional costly rework.

Moreover, while DHS's various governance bodies are generally following leading practices, they rely on data that are sometimes incomplete or inaccurate. Thus, it is important that DHS ensure that oversight decisions are based on complete and accurate program data. Until DHS's governance bodies are regularly provided complete and accurate data for use in their performance monitoring and oversight duties, its oversight decisions may be based on incorrect or outdated data and, therefore, may be flawed or of limited effectiveness.

Recommendations for Executive Action

To improve DHS's efforts to develop and implement its TECS Mod programs, we recommend that the Secretary of Homeland Security direct the CBP Commissioner to ensure that the appropriate individuals take the following four actions:

1. develop an integrated master schedule that accurately reflects all of the program's work activities, as well as the timing, sequencing, and dependencies between them;

2. ensure that all significant risks associated with the TECS Mod acquisition are documented in the program's risk and issue inventory inventory—including acquisition risks mentioned in this report report— and are briefed to senior management, as appropriate;

3. revise and implement the TECS Mod program's risk management strategy and guidance to include clear thresholds for when to escalate risks to senior management, and implement as appropriate; and

4. revise and implement the TECS Mod program's requirements management guidance to include the validation of requirements to ensure that each is unique, unambiguous, and testable.

We further recommend that the Secretary of Homeland Security direct the Acting Director of ICE to ensure that the appropriate individuals take the following three actions:

1. ensure that all significant risks associated with the TECS Mod acquisition are documented in the program's risk and issue inventory—including the acquisition risks mentioned in this report—and briefed to senior management, as appropriate;

2. revise and implement the TECS Mod program's risk management strategy and guidance to include clear thresholds for when to escalate risks to senior management, and implement as appropriate; and

3. ensure that the newly developed requirements management guidance and recently revised guidance for controlling changes to requirements are fully implemented.

We also recommend that the Secretary of Homeland Security direct the Under Secretary for Management and acting Chief Information Officer to ensure that data used by the department's governance and oversight bodies to assess the progress and performance of major IT program acquisition programs are complete, timely, and accurate.

Agency Comments and Our Evaluation

In written comments on a draft of this report, DHS agreed with seven of our recommendations and disagreed with one. The department described actions planned and underway to address the seven recommendations, and noted that it is committed to continuing its work toward full operational capability of its TECS Mod programs to enhance functionality for CBP, ICE, and other departments and agencies that have access to the system. The department also provided technical comments, which we incorporated as appropriate.

Regarding our recommendation that CBP develop an integrated master schedule that accurately reflects all of the program's work activities, as well as the timing, sequencing, and dependencies between them, DHS stated that CBP's Office of Information and Technology believes that the current master schedule in use provides the requisite amount of visibility into program work activities, and that it considers the program's scheduling efforts to be sound. Further, DHS stated that the timing and sequencing of TECS Mod's key activities, as well as the dependencies of activities, are tracked via the program schedule. We do not agree that CBP's current schedule provides either adequate visibility into program work activities, or that it includes the logical sequence of all key work activities, as well as the dependencies among them. As we state in our report, CBP had yet to define a detailed schedule for significant portions of the program. Moreover, approximately 65 percent of CBP's remaining work activities were not linked to other associated work activities; therefore the program's critical path could not be determined. As a result of these weaknesses, management is unable to determine how a slip in the completion date of a particular task may affect the overall project schedule. DHS also stated that CBP's schedule is reviewed bi-weekly at integrated project team meetings, as well as monthly at the CIO program management reviews to track status and upcoming milestones. However, given the issues with the schedule reflected in this report, using the current, incomplete schedule to track progress is not effective.

While DHS concurred with our recommendation that it ensure that data used by the department's governance and oversight bodies to assess the progress and performance of major IT program acquisitions are complete, timely, and accurate, DHS stated that it has already taken such steps, citing its enterprise Decision Support Tool, the DHS Investment Management System, and the reporting of program cost, schedule, and operation performance information on the Information Technology Dashboard. On this basis, DHS requested that the recommendation be considered resolved and closed. However, while we acknowledge that these tools are currently in place, we identified instances where DHS governance and oversight bodies were acting on information that was not complete, timely, or accurate, despite the presence of the tools and systems cited by DHS in its response. As we go forward with our follow-up activities for this report, we plan to monitor DHS's progress in improving the quality of data used in its assessments of major IT acquisition programs.

Finally, DHS stated that our draft report did not adequately recognize the progress made by CBP's TECS Mod program, specifically citing the strength of the program's risk and requirements management practices and schedule, as well as the fact that the program has already implemented certain functionality. We did report that (certain weaknesses notwithstanding) CBP's approach to risk and requirements management was generally consistent with leading practices. However, we also found significant deficiencies with CBP's master schedule for TECS Mod. Further, we noted that the Secondary Inspection project was already operational at air and sea ports of entry across the country, and was operational at land ports of entry by September 2013 - approximately 6 months earlier than estimated. We also revised the report to reflect that a portion of the modernized High Performance Primary Query Service are currently in use to recognize additional CBP progress.

As agreed with your offices, unless you publicly announce the contents of this report earlier, we plan no further distribution until 30 days from the report date. At that time, we will send copies to interested congressional committees and the Secretary of Homeland Security. This report will also be available at no charge on our website at http://www.gao.gov.

If you or your staffs have any questions on matters discussed in this report, please contact me at (202) 512-9286 or pownerd@gao.gov. Contact points for our Offices of Congressional Relations and Public Affairs may be found on the last page of this report. GAO staff who made major contributions to this report are listed in appendix V.

David A. Powner
Director, Information Technology
Management Issues

Appendix I: Objectives, Scope, and Methodology

The objectives of our review were to (1) determine the scope and status of the two Department of Homeland Security (DHS) TECS Modernization (TECS Mod) programs, (2) assess selected Customs and Border Protection (CBP) and Immigration and Customs Enforcement (ICE) program management practices for TECS Mod, and (3) assess the extent to which DHS is executing effective executive oversight and governance of the two TECS Mod programs.

To address our first objective, we reviewed a range of documentation from both programs, including each program's functional requirements documents; their respective acquisition program baselines and associated program cost and schedule estimates; program planning documents, such as program management plans and test and evaluation master plans; as well as the results of oversight reviews of both programs from July 2011 to June 2013. To assess the scope of each program, we determined what functionality each program had committed to provide, and analyzed pertinent documentation, such as program management plans, mission needs statements, concept of operations documents, and operational requirements documents (among others) to determine whether those commitments had changed over time. We also compared the schedule and cost commitments listed in the programs' initial documentation with subsequent baselines to establish the degree to which each program and its component subprojects had experienced changes in their start dates, completion dates, and estimated costs. Further, we corroborated statements made by CBP officials regarding the lack of completeness in their program master schedules by reviewing the completeness of their master schedule. Specifically, we examined the relationships that CBP documented (defined) between work activities within its master schedule for each project and the program overall. We used spreadsheet formulas to calculate what percentage of work activities linked to other work activities, and what percentage did not. We also interviewed relevant DHS officials to clarify and/or confirm information in the documents we reviewed and to more fully understand each program's scope and status.

To address our second objective, we examined program documentation, such as risk management and requirements management plans and processes, and compared them to relevant guidance from leading practitioners.

- **Risk management**: We compared relevant documentation, such as the CBP TECS Modernization Risk Management Plan and the ICE TECS Modernization Risk Management Plan, to relevant risk management guidance[1] to identify any variances. We focused on the extent to which: (1) a risk management strategy had been established, (2) roles and responsibilities for risk management activities had been defined and assigned, (3) a risk inventory has been created that includes plans for mitigating risks, and (4) the status of risks and mitigation efforts is regularly tracked. We also reviewed lists of identified risks found in risk inventories, and minutes from meetings at which risks were identified, monitored, and closed. We compared risks identified by us during the course of our work to the risks in the risk inventories to determine the extent to which all key risks were being actively managed. We also reviewed briefings provided at executive steering committee meetings to ascertain the extent to which program risks were disclosed at these reviews. Further, we discussed actions recently taken and planned to improve risk management activities within both CBP and ICE. To assess the reliability of the risk tools, we analyzed the nature and quality of access controls for both the CBP and ICE risk inventories to ensure that the data in the inventories were reliable for our purposes. To assess the reliability of the information in the risk inventories we used in this report, we interviewed knowledgeable agency officials about the nature and quality of controls over both the CBP and ICE inventories, and reviewed the information in the inventories to identify missing or invalid data entries. We found that sufficient controls were in place, and we therefore determined that the information is sufficiently reliable.

- **Requirements management**: We compared relevant requirements management documentation, such as the CBP TECS Mod Requirements Management Plan, the Passenger Systems Program Office's Change Management Process and Procedure, the ICE TECS Modernization Requirements Management Plan, and the ICE Change Control Board Standard Operating Procedure, to relevant requirements development and management guidance[2] to identify any variances. We focused on the extent to which: (1) a process for developing and managing requirements had been established; (2) roles and responsibilities for requirements management practices had been defined and assigned; (3) user needs had been elicited, translated into requirements, and then analyzed to ensure that each requirement was unique, unambiguous, and testable; and (4) a

---

[1] *CMMI for Development*, version 1.3.

[2] *CMMI for Development*, version 1.3.

change control process had been defined. We analyzed agency
documentation showing the implementation of these activities,
including evidence of requirements elicitation, analyses, review, and
approval, as well as examples of change request documents. We
interviewed program officials regarding the reasons for variances
between the guidance and documentation and the status of actions
recently taken and planned to improve requirements management
activities within both CBP and ICE.

To address our third objective, we analyzed documentation including
executive steering committee meetings results, and reviewed program
assessments from DHS's Office of the Chief Information Officer and
DHS's Program Accountability and Risk Management office, and
compared the results to relevant guidance such as our Information
Technology Investment Management Framework[3] to determine the extent
to which DHS is providing effective executive oversight and guidance to
the two TECS Mod programs. In addition, we compared the outputs of
these governance structures (such as briefing slides, meeting minutes,
and action items) to the ESC charters, and compared reports and
assessments prepared by DHS governance bodies to DHS's guidance for
conducting such assessments. We also interviewed relevant officials from
CBP, ICE, and DHS, as appropriate.

We conducted this performance audit from December 2012 to September
2013 in accordance with generally accepted government auditing
standards. Those standards require that we plan and perform the audit to
obtain sufficient, appropriate evidence to provide a reasonable basis for
our findings and conclusions based on our audit objectives. We believe
that the evidence obtained provides a reasonable basis for our findings
and conclusions based on our audit objectives.

---

[3]GAO, *Information Technology Investment Management: A Framework for Assessing and
Improving Process Maturity, Version 1.1*, GAO-04-394G (Washington, D.C.: March 2004).

Appendix II: Comments from the Department of Homeland Security

U.S. Department of Homeland Security
Washington, DC 20528

Homeland Security

November 12, 2013

David A. Powner
Director, Information Technology Management Issues
U.S. Government Accountability Office
441 G Street, NW
Washington, DC 20548

Re: Draft Report GAO-14-62, "BORDER SECURITY: DHS's Efforts to Modernize Key Enforcement Systems Could Be Strengthened"

Dear Mr. Powner:

Thank you for the opportunity to review and comment on this draft report. The U.S. Department of Homeland Security (DHS) appreciates the U.S. Government Accountability Office's (GAO's) work in planning and conducting its review and issuing this report.

The Department is pleased to note GAO's positive acknowledgement that DHS's Components have taken actions to oversee the two TECS Modernization (TECS Mod) programs; specifically, they have monitored TECS Mod performance and progress and have ensured that corrective actions have been identified and tracked. DHS is committed to continuing its work toward full operational capability of its TECS Mod Programs to enhance functionality for U.S. Customs and Border Protection (CBP), U.S. Immigration and Customs Enforcement (ICE), and other departments and agencies that have access to the system.

DHS, however, does not believe the report adequately recognizes some of the significant progress the CBP TECS Mod Program has made to date. While program planning and execution can always be improved, CBP TECS Mod has strong schedule, risk, and requirements management in place, which have helped deliver functionality to end users in four of the five major functional areas to date. The Program Management Office (PMO) has grown in staff and matured processes, while working closely with DHS offices since the program began in 2008. The modernized Secondary Inspection (SI) application was developed and deployed to a limited number of Air and Sea Ports of Entry (POEs) in 2009. It was fully deployed to all Air and Sea POEs in 2011 and fully deployed to all Land POEs in 2013. The modernized High Performance Primary Query Service was made operational in 2012 and is being used by the Advanced Passenger Information System. The user-facing functionality scheduled for delivery in 2013, including lookout and travel document queries, is active on the new TECS Portal (the face of modernized TECS), and more functionality will be provided in 2014, as planned.

Regarding the ICE TECS Mod Program, DHS agrees that more progress needs to be made in deploying this modernized case management system. ICE has taken action to revise its strategy and more clearly define the cost and schedule for discontinuing the use of legacy TECS information technology (IT) mainframe system by Fiscal Year 2015.

The draft report contained eight recommendations, seven with which the Department concurs (Recommendations 2 through 8) and one of which it non-concurs (Recommendation 1). Specifically, GAO recommended that the Secretary of Homeland Security:

Recommendation 1: Direct the CBP Commissioner to develop an integrated master schedule that accurately reflects all of the program's work activities, as well as the timing, sequencing, and dependencies between them.

Response: Non-concur. CBP's Office of Information and Technology (OIT) believes the current master schedule in use does provide the requisite amount of visibility into program and project activities and considers its scheduling efforts and process to be sound. CBP is continually improving the program and refining information in the schedule, as a result of project and program maturity. The timing and sequencing of key activities, as well as the dependencies of activities, are tracked via the schedule. The schedule is reviewed bi-weekly at TECS Modernization Integrated Project Team meetings and once a month at the CBP Chief Information Officer Program Management reviews to track status and upcoming milestones. CBP works continuously to ensure that the schedule management processes and techniques mitigate the constraints seen in MS Project to ensure that the Acquisition Program Baseline milestones, decision gates, and major deliverables continue to be managed and delivered within Program delivery dates. Given these actions, DHS requests that this recommendation be considered resolved and closed.

Recommendation 2: Direct the CBP Commissioner to ensure that all significant risks associated with the TECS Mod acquisition are documented in the program's risk and issue inventory - including the acquisition risks mentioned in this report - and are briefed to senior management, as appropriate.

Response: Concur. CBP OIT will include appropriate risks and/or issues in the risk register to include the acquisition risks identified in this report and will brief risks, as appropriate, during Program Management Review and Executive Steering Committee meetings. Estimated Completion Date (ECD): March 31, 2014.

Recommendation 3: Direct the CBP Commissioner revise and implement the TECS Mod program's risk management strategy and guidance to include clear thresholds for when to escalate risks to senior management, and implement as appropriate.

2

Response: Concur: CBP OIT will update the TECS Modernization Risk Management Plan (RMP) to include clearer guidance on when risks and issues should be escalated to the Passenger Systems Program Directorate Executive Director and higher for resolution, as appropriate. ECD: March 31, 2014.

Recommendation 4: Direct the CBP Commissioner revise and implement the TECS Mod program's requirements management guidance to include the validation of requirements to ensure that each is unique, unambiguous, and testable.

Response: Concur. CBP OIT will update the TECS Mod RMP to include the words "unique, unambiguous, and testable" when describing good requirement characteristics. ECD: December 31, 2013.

Recommendation 5: Direct the Acting Director of ICE to ensure that all significant risks associated with the TECS Mod acquisition are documented in the program's risk and issue inventory-including the acquisition risks mentioned in this report-and briefed to senior management, as appropriate.

Response: Concur. The ICE TECS Mod PMO will update the Risk and Issue Register to include all significant risks and escalate them to senior management as they are identified in a timely manner. In regard to acquisition risks mentioned in the report, the program currently has an open risk related to discontinuing the use of legacy TECS by 2015 in its Risk and Issue Register. The program will open and brief a new risk related to the management and usability of requirements. ECD: December 31, 2013.

Recommendation 6: Direct the Acting Director of ICE to revise and implement the TECS Mod program's risk management strategy and guidance to include clear thresholds for when to escalate risks to senior management, and implement, as appropriate.

Response: Concur. The ICE TECS Mod PMO will establish clear thresholds for escalating risks to senior management. Specifically, the PMO will update its Risk Management Plan to clearly document the threshold criteria and incorporate it into its risk management process. ECD: January 31, 2014.

Recommendation 7: Direct the Acting Director of ICE to ensure that the newly developed requirements management guidance and recently revised guidance for controlling changes to requirements are fully implemented.

Response: Concur. The ICE TECS Mod PMO has fully implemented its Requirements Management and Change Control processes. The program is currently reviewing and refining its

3

more than 19,000 detailed requirements to be focused on functionality (i.e., "what") rather than design (i.e., "how") as well as maintain a manageable level. The program is planning to have the requirements refined by December 2013. All requirement changes will go through the approved Change Control process. ECD: December 31, 2013.

Recommendation 8: Direct the Under Secretary for Management and the Acting Chief Information Officer to ensure that data used by the department's governance and oversight bodies to assess the progress and performance of major IT program acquisition programs are complete, timely, and accurate.

Response: Concur. DHS has taken steps to ensure that the data used by the IT program acquisition programs are accurate, complete, and timely. Specifically, on February 13, 2012, the Under Secretary for Management issued a memorandum that directed the implementation of an enterprise Decision Support Tool (DST). The DST is designed to improve DHS's governance capabilities and aid departmental strategic acquisition decision making, and ensures consistency in reporting and consolidation of data from various systems into a single view. Additionally, the Information Technology Dashboard, which receives data from the DHS Investment Management System (IMS), improves transparency and oversight of IT investments and provides DHS oversight and governance bodies with the ability to track the progress of major IT investments over time. Program Managers must provide investment updates each month in IMS. Updates include project and activity cost, schedule and operational metric performance information, project and operational risks, and cost and schedule variance information for each major investment.

In light of above, DHS requests this recommendation be considered resolved and closed on the basis of supporting documentation, provided under separate cover, that demonstrates the Department has implemented actions to ensure the data used are complete, timely, and accurate.

Again, thank you for the opportunity to review and provide comments on this draft report. Technical comments were previously provided under separate cover. Please feel free to contact me if you have any questions. We look forward to working with you in the future.

Sincerely,

Jim H. Crumpacker
Director
Departmental GAO-OIG Liaison Office

4

Appendix III: Description of Key Systems and Data on Legacy TECS

TECS is a border enforcement system that supports the sharing of information about people seeking entry into the country. The system interfaces with several law enforcement systems and federal agencies, and supports the screening of people and conveyances who are inadmissible or may pose a threat to the country. In addition, it provides an investigative case management function for activities including money-laundering tracking and reporting; telephone data analysis; and intelligence reporting and dissemination. The following table provides a description of key systems and data associated with the passenger screening processes within TECS.

Table 6: Subsystems and Data Available through TECS

Subsystem	Owner	Description
Data that resides on TECS and is collected by CBP		
Advance Passenger Information System	CBP	Database that contains the biographical information collected by air carriers and sea vessels on passengers and crew members. The information is collected in advance of a passenger's departure from or arrival into (and in many cases, prior to departure for) the United States. This information collection also assists in expediting processing of travelers at ports of entry, resulting in a significant time savings.
Border Crossing Information System	CBP	Database used to receive and maintain border crossing information on travelers who are admitted or paroled into or departing from the United States, this information includes: certain biographical information; a photograph; certain itinerary information provided by air and sea carriers and any other forms of passenger transportation, including rail, which is or may subsequently be mandated, or is or may be provided on a voluntary basis; and the time and location of the border crossing.
Global Enrollment System	CBP	Database that contains information on the enrollment and vetting processes for trusted traveler and registered traveler programs in a centralized environment, currently includes Global Entry trusted traveler program.
Non-immigrant Information System	CBP	Database that includes information from the forms filled out by nonimmigrant aliens entering the United States. Includes length of stay and departure data.
Seized Asset and Case Tracking System	CBP	Database that documents individuals and businesses who violated laws or provided assistance in identifying or locating those who have violated laws and collects and maintains records on fines and penalties.
Data that resides on TECS but is not collected by CBP		
Interface with U.S. Department of State: Passport Information Electronic Records System	Department of State	Database that includes passport information (e.g., the applicant's surname, date of birth, address, telephone number, and social security number), other personal identifying information (e.g., driver's license or other identifying number(s), and identifiable information, such as educational, financial, employment, and medical information).

Subsystem	Owner	Description
Interface with U.S. Department of State: Consular Consolidated Database	Department of State	Database that contains over 100 million visa cases and 75 million photographs including names, addresses, birthdates, biometric data, race, identification numbers, and country of origin.
Interface with Non-Federal Entity Data System	CBP	This system supports certain travel documents, such as Enhanced Driver's Licenses, issued by other government authorities, such as states or Canadian provinces or Canadian territories, that agree to provide CBP with a copy of the database storing biographical information and a photograph pertaining to each document holder in advance of the traveler crossing the border.
Interface with U.S. Citizenship and Information Services: Alien File and Central Index System	USCIS	Central Index System contains information on the status of 57 million applicants/petitioners seeking immigration benefits to include: lawful permanent residents, naturalized citizens, U.S. border crossers, aliens who illegally entered the United States, aliens who have been issued employment authorization documents, individuals who petitioned for benefits on behalf of family members, and other individuals subject to the provisions of the Immigration and Nationality Act. Central Index System also tracks the location of paper case files, known as A-files.
Interface with the DHS Watchlist Service	DHS	Watchlist data include the biographical and biometric data of known or suspected terrorists for the purposes of national security. Information includes name, date of birth, place of birth, biometric or photographic data, passport and/or driver's license information, and other available identifying particulars used to compare the identify of an individual being screened with a known or suspected terrorist.
Data that is accessible through TECS but does not reside on TECS		
National Crime Information Center	FBI	This is an FBI system that includes criminal record history information on persons by law enforcement agencies throughout the United States and internationally. It contains information on stolen property, wanted persons, missing persons, violent gangs and terrorists, and other persons of interest to law enforcement. It is also a conduit to a database of over 54 million criminal history records.
NLETS (formerly known as the National Law Enforcement Telecommunications System)	State and local law enforcement	Provides access to state and local law enforcement information, such as criminal and driver records.
California Law Enforcement Telecommunications System	State of California	Similar to NLETS, this system provides access to California-specific law information, such as criminal and driver records.
Canadian Police Information Center	Canada	This system is the national repository of police information that amounts to a vital shared resource within Canadian law enforcement.

Source: GAO analysis of DHS data.

Appendix IV: Description of CBP's Five TECS Modernization Projects

CPB plans to deliver the following capabilities incrementally across five projects by September 2015. Specifically,

- Secondary Inspection: This project is to support processing of travelers referred from primary inspection for either enforcement or administrative reasons.[1] The modernized version of Secondary Inspection, according to CBP, is to streamline the processing of encounters by eliminating the need for users to navigate through complex system menus to perform tasks, and minimize redundant data entry,[2] as well as to simplify the interface so that all of the information is presented on a single screen. This project is to also provide web-based interface access to information such as relevant laws, policies, and forensics. In addition, this project is to provide a means to record the outcome of each inspection. According to CBP, Secondary Inspection is currently operational at all air, land, and sea ports of entry.[3]
- High Performance Primary Query and Manifest Processing: This project is intended to improve TECS data search results in order to expedite the processing of manifests[4] from individuals traveling to the United States on commercial or private aircraft, and commercial vessels. CBP plans to migrate the mainframe-based lookout records and other data to the modernized infrastructure, and replace the 1980s era databases and queries with modernized tools for the primary inspection process. It is to be fully operational by March 2015.
- Travel Document and Encounter Data: This project is intended to improve CBP's ability to query and validate travel documentation for both passengers and their means of conveyance (whether people enter the country by air, sea, or land—by foot or in a vehicle). It is intended to modernize existing travel document data presented during

---

[1] The primary inspection process is the first part of the inspection process where CBP officers interviews travelers and inspects their travel documents to determine if they may be admitted or should be referred for further questioning and document examination. If additional review is necessary, the traveler is referred to secondary inspection where another officer makes a final determination to admit or deny admission.

[2] In the existing system, the information required by secondary inspectors is spread across three different applications embedded within TECS, each of which requires a separate sign-on.

[3] Ports of entry are government-designated locations where CBP inspects persons and goods to determine whether they may be lawfully admitted into the country.

[4] A manifest is a list of passengers or an invoice of cargo for a vehicle or vessel (like a ship or plane).

primary and secondary inspections. It will also provide web-based interfaces intended to allow quick access to a passenger's complete travel history, while also implementing appropriate data access restrictions and privacy protections in compliance with agencies' data policies. It is to be fully operational by March 2015.

- Lookout Record Data and Screening Services: This project is intended to improve the efficiency of existing data screening and analyses capabilities by providing a means to quickly create, update, and send and receive lookout record data to external agencies, such as the law enforcement community. It is to be fully operational by March 2015.

- Primary Inspection Processes: This project is intended to modernize the overall inspection process and provide support for additional or random screening and communication functions. CBP states that this project will upgrade lookout record alarms and alerts sent to air, sea, and land primary and secondary workstations to ensure the safety of inspection officers. In addition, the project will modernize the user interfaces for alternate inspections—any inspection that is not conducted at an air, sea, vehicle, or pedestrian primary inspection location. It is to be fully operational by March 2015.

Appendix V: GAO Contact and Staff Acknowledgments

GAO Contact	David A. Powner, (202) 512-9286 or pownerd@gao.gov
Staff Acknowledgments	In addition to the contact name above, individuals making contributions to this report included Deborah Davis (Assistant Director), Kara Epperson, Rebecca Eyler, Daniel Gordon, Dave Hinchman (Assistant Director), Sandra Kerr, Jamelyn Payan, and Jessica Waselkow.

GAO's Mission	The Government Accountability Office, the audit, evaluation, and investigative arm of Congress, exists to support Congress in meeting its constitutional responsibilities and to help improve the performance and accountability of the federal government for the American people. GAO examines the use of public funds; evaluates federal programs and policies; and provides analyses, recommendations, and other assistance to help Congress make informed oversight, policy, and funding decisions. GAO's commitment to good government is reflected in its core values of accountability, integrity, and reliability.
Obtaining Copies of GAO Reports and Testimony	The fastest and easiest way to obtain copies of GAO documents at no cost is through GAO's website (http://www.gao.gov). Each weekday afternoon, GAO posts on its website newly released reports, testimony, and correspondence. To have GAO e-mail you a list of newly posted products, go to http://www.gao.gov and select "E-mail Updates."
Order by Phone	The price of each GAO publication reflects GAO's actual cost of production and distribution and depends on the number of pages in the publication and whether the publication is printed in color or black and white. Pricing and ordering information is posted on GAO's website, http://www.gao.gov/ordering.htm. Place orders by calling (202) 512-6000, toll free (866) 801-7077, or TDD (202) 512-2537. Orders may be paid for using American Express, Discover Card, MasterCard, Visa, check, or money order. Call for additional information.
Connect with GAO	Connect with GAO on Facebook, Flickr, Twitter, and YouTube. Subscribe to our RSS Feeds or E-mail Updates. Listen to our Podcasts. Visit GAO on the web at www.gao.gov.
To Report Fraud, Waste, and Abuse in Federal Programs	Contact: Website: http://www.gao.gov/fraudnet/fraudnet.htm E-mail: fraudnet@gao.gov Automated answering system: (800) 424-5454 or (202) 512-7470
Congressional Relations	Katherine Siggerud, Managing Director, siggerudk@gao.gov, (202) 512-4400, U.S. Government Accountability Office, 441 G Street NW, Room 7125, Washington, DC 20548
Public Affairs	Chuck Young, Managing Director, youngc1@gao.gov, (202) 512-4800 U.S. Government Accountability Office, 441 G Street NW, Room 7149 Washington, DC 20548

Please Print on Recycled Paper.